MW00464815

Susanne Jönsson
Activate you Merkaba and reach a Higher Consciousness
copyright © 2021, Susanne Jönsson
www.soulheartjourney.com
Published by HC-Publishing

ISBN 978-91-87807-16-9

How to activate your Merkaba and reach a Higher Consciousness

By Susanne Jönsson

Do you prefer video and Mp3 instructions? You'll find most of these exercises on:

www.soulheartjourney.com

Soul&Heart
Journey School

Index

It´s time!

I have found practical techniques to achieve a Higher Consciousness and a Heart Consciousness. I understand how important it is to teach these techniques to as many as possible.

My goal is that everyone should have an opportunity to learn – or remember- how to reach a Heart Consciousness.

Being able to train in these techniques over a relatively short time is a great advantage, most of us have been working for many years to reach the equivalent knowledge, but my belief is that it is now, in the times we live in, we need this knowledge! It's time!

Reach your true I am and your true potential by working towards a Higher Consciousness.

This gives you balance and a key to harmony, focus and freedom on many levels.

5

About the author

Founder of Soul & Heart Journey School

Therapist, Healer, Teacher and Author

"We all carry all wisdom and knowledge inside ourselves all the time. The challenge is how to reach this inner knowledge and how to use and apply it in the most effective way.
At Soul & Heart Journey School you will learn this and more." (Susanne Jönsson)

Susanne Jönsson is a certified holistic therapist & teacher, from Sweden, with more than 20 years of professional work experience.

Her passion is to help people to live from their hearts and find their inner knowledge.

From brain consciousness to Heart Consciousness

.

This E-book is designed to help you reach higher levels of your consciousness.

It will give you a straight and clear path to follow and gives you techniques that you need to reach the fourth dimension, where we all are headed.

The technique I will use in this course is based on gaining more knowledge about our light bodies, about other sacred parts of ourselves and how to activate or reach them with the aid of various techniques and/or meditations.

These techniques have for the most part been hidden from the general public but now the time is right for everyone who wants to take part of this knowledge to gain access and find their way towards a Higher Consciousness.

Chapter 1 - The foundations of meditations

To simplify things, there are essentially three different meditation techniques.

The first one is sometimes called experience meditation. Here you are supposed to experience something special during the meditation, maybe climb a mountain, meet a guide, or even receive inner guidance or something similar.

The second one consists of clearing out your thoughts to make a free space in your head. Using this technique, you often chant a Mantra to clear your thoughts. This is the most common way of meditation where you create inner peace.

The third one consists of consciously making an effort to reach a Higher Consciousness. This is the type of meditation we will be working with in this on-line course. Here you will learn techniques which have been hidden from mankind for thousands of years and in some cases, you will learn techniques used by the monks in Tibet, earned by hard discipline during a period of some twelve different incarnations before they were entitled to receive the full knowledge. The reason this knowledge is available today is that we all live in a higher frequency on this earth and that all men can therefore access these ancient techniques in a safe and grounded way. We should, of course, have a deep respect for our actions and we should be aware, as we take each new step, that everything feels right and balanced.

Heart Meditation and Love Meditation

These two meditation techniques are the foundations you need to learn. You decide yourself the actual length of these meditations. If you are in a hurry you can perform them in 5 minutes but preferably you should initially allow 15-20 minutes. Do these meditations at least twice a week but if you have the opportunity you will greatly benefit by doing them on a daily basis.

Heart Meditation

In this meditation you should anchor your heart into the Earth and the Sun. You will be sending your love to Them and you will feel how both the Earth and the Sun send Their love back to you and to each other. In this way you will be creating and experiencing a trinity of love between the mother (Earth), the father (Sun) and the child (which is you). Feel this love radiate and fill all parts of you with love.

Heart Meditation – to anchor the heart into the Earth and the Sun

Sit comfortably with your feet firmly placed on the floor or stand up if this suits you better.

Inhale a few deep breaths and close your eyes

Imagine yourself standing in a beautiful place here on earth, a place that you love and where you feel secure. It can be a forest or by a lake or up in the mountains. Choose a place you like the most and observe all the details.

Feel how your love of the Mother Earth grows and grows, feel how your heart opens and feel how your love to the Mother Earth radiates outwards from your heart.

You are now creating a sphere (a globe) containing your love to the Mother Earth. Transport this sphere of love deep down into the Earth and allow Her to receive your love.

Soon you will feel the response from the Mother, you will feel Her love for you. Her love fills all parts of you – sit in Her field of love for a while.

Turn your gaze towards the night sky. You see all the stars and planets and you are filled with your love to the Father. Feel how your love grows and grows, how your heart opens and how your love to the Father is radiating outwards.

You are now creating a sphere (a globe) containing your love to the Father. Transport this sphere of love high up, up into the Sun Itself and allow Him to receive your love.

Soon you will feel the response from the Father, you will feel His love for you. His love fills all parts of you – sit in the Father's field of love for a while.

Now you will also see how the Father and the Mother send their love to each other and you will see how you all together form a trinity of love. The Mother, the Father and the holy Child. This child is you. Together you are now creating the original holy trinity. Feel the essence of love radiating between the three of you. Sit in this field of love for a while.

When it is time to finish the meditation, you should first move your hands and your body. Then when you are ready, open your eyes and finish the meditation.

Love Meditation

In this meditation you create an inner understanding that we are all one and that everything we do affects each other. When you can feel and understand the importance of being in the energy field that brings you well-being, then you will also appreciate that it concerns us all.

Sit comfortably with your feet firmly placed on the floor and the palms of the hands facing down on the knees.

Repeat silently to yourself:

I am Love (see how you radiate love and become like the inner core of a flower)

All are Love (see how everyone around you are like petals in the flower and radiate the same love)

We are One (see how you all together form a large flower)

We are Love (see how this flower radiates the same love)

I am Love (see how your "I Am" becomes the flower)

All are Love (see how large your environment has become; new and larger petals in the flower radiating the same love)

We are One (see how you all together form a very large flower)

We are Love (see how this flower is radiating the same love)

Repeat the meditation and let your "I Am" – your flower – grow more and more. Soon you will be covering large areas of the Earth – continue until you reach round the globe, until your "I Am"/flower and its petals encompass the whole Planet and you see or feel how the whole Planet is radiating with love.

This is Oneness Consciousness or Unity. Sit in this feeling for a while.

Wishing you success!

The formation of the Light Bodies

There are many varied parts of our Light Bodies available to us today. In this course we will concentrate on the parts of our Light Bodies that we can activate and use in our work towards a Higher Consciousness.

First I want to show you the various parts we will be working with.

The Crown

This Light Body is situated around our head. About 2000 years ago it was common to see this active crown on enlightened people depicted in paintings. It is the same principle we call a halo.

It is very important that you follow the activation exactly as described. This exercise should be repeated every day for two weeks. After this period the crown is activated and ready.

The technique you will be using is the same technique that is used globally to activate the crown in order to reach a Higher Consciousness.

An activated crown seen in frontal position.

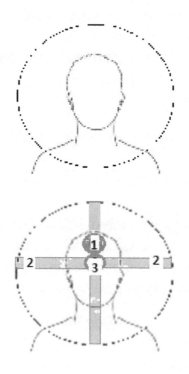

The "rays" radiating from the crown have lost their contact with the pineal gland since a long time ago and therefore the rays have decreased considerably in size. The picture below shows how the rays look on most people today when the crown is not activated.

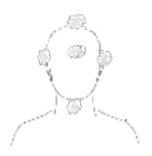

Merkaba

This word exists in most languages around the world and the meaning is always the same even if the exact word is somewhat different. Merkaba means a rotating light which carries the body and the spirit from one world to another, i.e. a Light Body which carries man to a Higher Consciousness. In lessons 3, 4 and 5 we will explain and work with the activation of your Merkaba.

This is what a Merkaba field looks like when you are close:

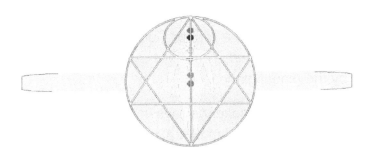

Merkaba field seen from a distance:

Merkaba field seen from a long distance:

20

Activate the Crown

The pineal gland is situated in the middle of your head. It connects the soul with the body and is largely underdeveloped in our bodies today. When a person develops a Higher Consciousness the pineal gland is activated. The "third eye" is also activated by the pineal gland.

Our task is to make the rays in the Crown grow and gain contact with the pineal gland again. It is very important that you perform this exercise exactly as it is described:

The Crown seen from the side

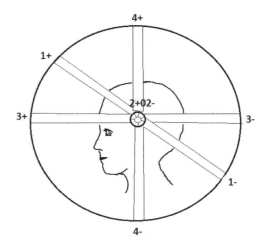

The Crown seen in frontal view

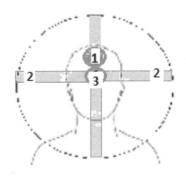

This is a practise you should perform on yourself and absolutely <u>not</u> on any other person! You can either perform the practise mentally or physically by doing the movements simultaneously.

Decide that you can actually see the pineal gland. Do not worry about if it works or not – just decide that you can do it! The pineal gland is often reddish in colour but sometimes it can take other hues.

Rays 1+ and 1- (refer to illustrations).
Place the left hand above the forehead 1+ (where you would have had a horn of a unicorn), keep the right hand on 1-.

Make one ray at a time grow and become larger (starting with 1+) until it reaches its correct size (see illustration). You make it grow by persuading the body to send out a stronger energy flow – increase until the power and strength feels right. Do the same with the next ray 1-.

Decide that you can look down onto your crown chakra and see the pineal gland. Now take one ray at a time and connect it firmly inside the pineal gland. The energy is of a light colour and quite sharp. You need to be clear in your intention to make the ray connect and keep it connected with the pineal gland, first 1+ and then 1-.

When both rays have connected, keep them so for at least ½-1 minutes. If you get tired, think that you "stand" (in your mind) on the left side of the body and do this in your mind instead.

Next you may start to feel the different pulses of the rays (like heart beats). Make them beat in unison. When they are doing this, count to at least 20 beats in unison before you let go.

Place yourself behind your body (in your mind) and repeat with the next couple of rays, 2+ and 2- (2+ is located on your left side- use left hand and 2- on your right – use right hand).

Place yourself on the left side again (in your mind) and repeat with rays 3+ and 3- (left hand front and right hand back).

You should not activate the rays 4+ and 4-. They will appear automatically once the others are established.

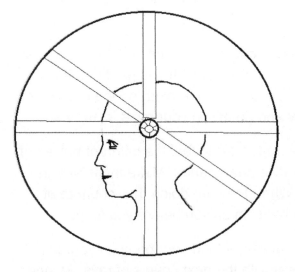

This exercise needs to be repeated every day for two weeks. After this period your Crown is activated for the rest of your life.

Although the Crown will be activated you can still, if you so wish, do this exercise later so that you may learn to get to know your Crown.
It is enough to make the whole exercise in 1 minute to quickly check that the Crown and the Rays are active.

Exercises for chapter 1

Learn how to anchor your Heart into the Earth and the Sun. It is good to start each day with this meditation.

Do the Love Meditation at least twice a week. Allow approx. 15-20 minutes each time.

Activate your Crown. This exercise should be done each day for two weeks consecutively to ensure that the Crown is securely activated.

You decide how much time you wish to spend on your exercises. My recommendation is that you follow the instructions given. It is not necessarily advantageous to do the exercises too many times and if not done enough times may delay your progress. You decide for yourself.

Next chapter is about reaching secret and sacred spaces within your heart.

Chapter 2 – Your Heart

If you have followed the instructions in chapter 1, you will now have activated the Crown for the rest of your life. You no longer need to do this activation exercise but sometimes your Crown may call for a bit more attention. You can then do the exercise again as it will increase your sense of well-being.

Hopefully you are enjoying your Heart Meditations. These will continue during the course and you should therefore look upon them with deep love.

In this chapter we will continue our journey into the body to find new important pathways towards your Higher Consciousness. We will work with the Sacred Space of the Heart.

In order to reach this space you need to understand that your mind is flexible. You can easily move your mind inside your body whenever you want to do so.

If you lean back and feel within your body, where is the seat of your mind?

Most people reply after a few moments that the mind lives behind your eyes and this is where our "conscious consciousness" is situated. In other words, this is where you experience your mind when you are looking for it inside your body.

You will now experience how you can wander about with your mind inside the body. You only need to do this exercise a couple of times before you proceed further.

Exercise, travel in your body

Read this instruction a couple of times. It is as short as possible to enable you to remember it while you are performing the exercise.

Sit comfortably with your feet firmly on the ground and the palms of your hands facing downwards, resting on your lap.

Close your eyes.

Tune into your mind, imagining it is located behind your eyes.

Feel the softness and warmth in this area

Decide that your mind is wandering downwards and decide that you can see the firm interior of your nose and cheek-bone.

Travel past the chin and continue down into the throat.

Stop for a while in the throat chakra and feel the soft structure surrounding your mind.

Wander slowly back again.

Do this exercise at least twice but continue repeating it until you understand how you can travel inside the body, then continue with the following exercise:

Exercise

Sit comfortably with your feet firmly on the ground and the palms of your hands facing downwards, resting on your lap.

Close your eyes.

Tune into your mind, imagining it is located behind your eyes.

Feel the softness and warmth in this area

Decide that your mind is wandering downwards and decide that you can see the firm interior of your nose and cheek-bone.

Travel past the chin and continue down into the throat.

Stop for a while in the throat chakra and feel the soft structure surrounding your mind.

Experience the feeling that your nose is high above you and your stomach below you.

Decide to continue travelling outwards into your right arm, feel and experience the arm from the inside all the way down into the hand.

Slowly travel backwards again into the throat chakra.

Now travel down your left arm and experience it from the inside and then continue down into the hand.

Slowly travel back into the throat chakra.

Then continue back up to the space behind the eyes.

The more you practice this exercise, the easier will be your next part.

Energy field – vortex field

As I was showing you in Lesson 1, our energy field consists of many parts, many different light bodies. These light bodies have different functions and different looks. The part of the light body we are going to examine now is the vortex field connected to our physical heart. This field is quite large and can be seen 1-2 meters outside the body of a person who is in balance. A vortex field is a field of circulating energy moving round, both vertically and horizontally.

Do you remember a toy that most of us played with as a child, a "Slinky"? It was a spinning spiral that could "climb" stairs. If you imagine this spiral and then turn the end bits towards each other so that you simultaneously make a circle within the spiral …

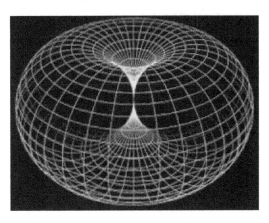

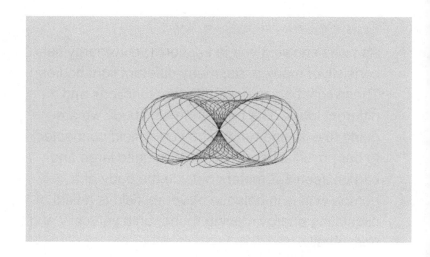

The easiest way to describe this is to show an illustration. Imagine how the energy is flowing from the inner core and out – turns and returns again. It is a flow of energy collecting and transmitting power from the same center.

Please read the following pages and page 21 first – do not attempt to do the exercise or experience at the same time. First you will need to grasp the general idea before you do the exercise.

Imagine that the source of the vortex field originates from your heart – from the Sacred Space in the Heart.

When you journey with your mind to the throat chakra (1) you can see the field of the vortex (2). You can follow the field of the vortex down to the Sacred Space of the Heart (3).

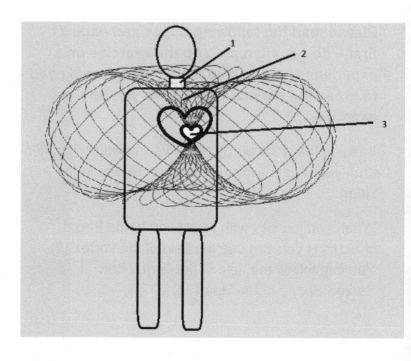

When you have access to the Sacred Space of the Heart, it will connect you with the Universe.

You can reach it via this vortex field. You need to use your will power and determination in order to decide that you are finding the right way.

 When you enter the Sacred Space of the Heart it is completely dark – you must first light the light by affirming "let there be light". You will then experience how light is surrounding you. Where this light source comes from varies. The first time you arrive in your Sacred Space, take a good look around.

After a while you will hear a tone, a sound.

You will hear "Ohm" or a sound that is just yours in your personal tone. Listen and enjoy.

When you have moved around your Sacred Space of the Heart you will eventually see a small passage.

When you enter this small space you will at the same time hear how the tone of the Ohm gets higher and becomes lighter.

Enter this space and sit down

Look up and you will see the whole galaxy surrounding you! You can see the same stars as you see outside of yourself in night.

You may remain in this space in peace for as long as you wish.

When it is time to return, leave your mind here – in this Room under the Stars – that will help you to live from your heart, even when life struggles.

This meditation is available in both videos and mp3 files for download if you think that will help.

It will guide you first how to anchor your heart in the sun and in the Earth and then how you find your sacred space in your heart.

You'll find them on: www.soulheartjourney.com

To find the Sacred Space of the Heart

(NOTE: Start by reading instructions how to anchor the Heart with the Crown)

Sit comfortably with your feet firmly on the ground and the palms of your hands facing downwards on your lap.

Become aware of your mind just behind your eyes.

Travel with your mind slowly downwards. Experience the feeling of moving around inside your body.

Reach down to your throat chakra and take a deep breath.

Become aware of the vortex field emanating from your heart.

Breathe!

Think: "let there be Light!" See how the light lights up your space. Know that everyone have their own way and their own light source.

Look around your space for a short while.

You will now hear the sound of Ohm, listen how it fills the whole space and feel how the vibration of the Ohm is filling your body.

After a while you will see or become aware of another small space, here in the Sacred Space of your Heart.

When you can see/feel this space you make your way there. It is a small space …

When you enter the space you will hear the frequency of the Ohm lifting to a higher level.

Sit down comfortably in this small space.

Become aware of being surrounded by the whole galaxy, see all the stars and planets. You will notice that they are the same as those you experience "outside" of yourself.

Move the tip of your tongue up towards the roof of your mouth

You are now connected to your God energy. Sit quietly in this divine experience for a while but no longer than 20 minutes.

When it is time to end the meditation, leave your mind here, and just move your fingers and feet a little bit. Then open your eyes.

Anchor the Heart with the Crown

There is an energy passage in your body enabling contact between your Heart and your Crown. It is a sacred passage which has not been accessible or known to us until now.

This passage goes via the mouth, the tip of your tongue and the roof of your mouth. Up in the roof of your mouth is a spot which becomes soft when you press it with the tip of your tongue. This spot activates a function in your brain which in turn influences the Pineal Gland. This gland will then produce a signal or energy which flows through your mind and gives you a high degree of well-being. It is not always easy to find the right spot in the roof of the mouth. You need to feel your way around until you experience this sense of well-being.

The simplest guidance I can give you is to feel with the tongue in the roof of the mount, feel where the teeth meet the gum. Move the tongue "up the hill" until you reach the roof of the mouth. The first part is rough/hard but then it becomes smooth and tight, then it is soft one more time.

Exactly between the area of smooth and soft and hard – this is where this spot is usually found.

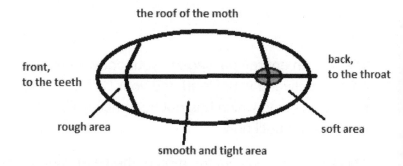

the roof of the moth

front,
to the teeth

back,
to the throat

rough area

soft area

smooth and tight area

Try several times until you find the right spot and you get good effect when you are close enough so keep on trying.

What is actually happening when you do this while being in the Sacred Space of your Heart is that you create an energy passage between the Heart and the Crown. This way you anchor the energy and raise your consciousness. The flow of energy you feel is Prana (life energy) which is activated and flows through your body. It is at this point where you start activating your Third Eye.

Exercises for chapter 2

Continue to anchor your Heart into the Earth and the Sun. It is good to start each day with this meditation.

Do the meditation to find The Sacred Space of the Heart at least twice a week, about 15-20 minutes each time.

Be particular with anchoring between the Heart and the Crown.

You decide how much time you wish to spend on your exercises. My recommendation is that you follow the instructions given. It is not necessarily advantageous to do the exercises too many times and if not done enough times may delay your progress. You decide for yourself.

Chapter 3 – The Star Tetrahedron

Now that you have gained access to the Sacred Space of Your Heart, I hope you will make sure to explore the first chamber thoroughly. In this chamber you will eventually gain great knowledge about yourself. Please do   not think that this is merely a distance to be travelled.

As time goes by, you will learn in this chamber how to interpret the symbols and signs written all over, on the walls, on pillars or wherever you can find them. Remember that your chamber is just *yours.* It is there for your private and personal development.

In this lesson we will start to activate your Merkaba. To begin with it may seem complicated but once you have learnt the technique it will appear quick and simple. Once you know the Merkaba meditation it will take less than 5 minutes daily to keep your Merkaba active.

The complete Merkaba meditation is done through 17 in-breaths. In this lesson No. 3 we will start by explaining the foundations of your Merkaba and practice the first 6 breathings.

Different sensations and touch will help you activate your Merkaba

There are several steps you need to take simultaneously during each in-breath. Initially I will explain the different parts and what you should think or do. Last I will assemble the various parts to enable you to start your Merkaba activation

Heart

Under this heading you will be instructed which feeling you should have in your heart during each part. It will vary between the different in-breaths so please take note. It is important to perform all the parts as correctly as possible.

Mind

Here is described what you should look at or visualise (determine that you will see).

Body

Here is described which movements you should perform – they vary between the different parts of the meditation.

Mudra

A Mudra is an ancient and holy energy movement performed with your fingers and hands. These movements will help you awaken your cell memories.

Breathing

The breathing is governing the process during the whole Merkaba meditation. It is therefore important that you perform the breathing exercises on the next page until you feel that your body recognises the way of breathing and thereby starts relaxing and assisting the meditation.

Breathing

First of all you need to understand how the breathing works.

When we breathe during the Merkaba meditation the breathing is done consciously and focused.

The breathing is often deeper than normal.

Each in-breath takes at least 7 seconds and the out-breath the same length of time.

Fill your inside with air in a gentle and comfortable way, long – gentle – deep in-breaths.

You inhale and even exhale mostly through your nose.

Each breath should feel comfortable inside your body. You should not strain your body with the intake of air but rather allow the air to find its natural place inside the body.

Breath exercise 1

Breathe deeply according to the above instructions. Try to make the in-breath and out-breath the same length of time. Do at least 10 breathing cycles.

Allow the in-breath to make you focused.

During the out-breath feel how you are exhaling all tension from your body.

Feel inside your body. Does the breathing feel comfortable? If so, good. You can now move on to the next exercise.

Do you experience tension in your chest or solar plexus? Continue to practise until you feel relaxed.

Exercise 2

Allow each in-breath to take at least 7 seconds and the out-breath the same length of time.

Practise until the breathing feels gentle, focused and conscious.

Practise until you can draw at least 17 in-breaths in this way.

Sacred Geometry

In the Sacred Geometry there are five basic shapes that can be traced in everything. Even the traditional geometry agrees on this. Sacred Geometry comprises shapes, tones and frequencies which can be shown in pictures but even numbers and colours.

During the Merkaba activation we will use shapes and we will use Fibonacci numbers. There is no room here to explain this more deeply. If you want to know more, I recommend that you start looking for information about Sacred Geometry, the Golden Mean and Fibonacci on the Internet or read The Ancient Secret of the Flower of Life, Vol. 1 and 2, as well as Living in the Heart by Drunvalo Melchizedek.

Briefly I will show you the five basic shapes which form the foundation for the whole of Creation.

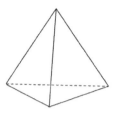

Tetrahedron

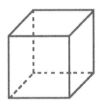

Hexahedron

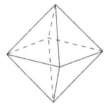

Octahedron

Icosahedron

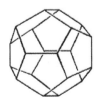

Dodecahedron

Tetrahedron star

Your inner Merkaba field consists of a Tetrahedron star – it is actually two Tetrahedrons brought together and through each other until they form a star.

The upper Tetrahedron is masculine (points towards the Sun)

The lower Tetrahedron is feminine (points towards the Earth)

Men and women each have their Tetrahedron turned in different directions – please note in the instruction which one applies to you.

When you experience your Merkaba it is important <u>that you see yourself from within the Merbaka.</u>

In other words, you should not look at yourself from the outside sitting in the Merkaba – **<u>you should experience the Merkaba from within! Practise until you are certain.</u>**

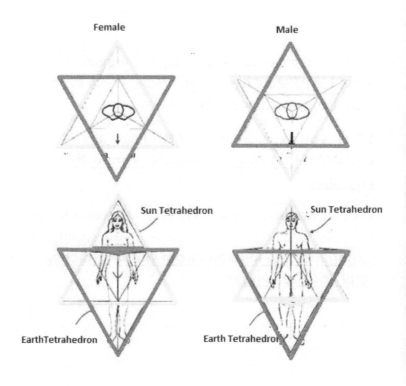

Female Male

Sun Tetrahedron

Sun Tetrahedron

EarthTetrahedron

Earth Tetrahedron

Women/female:

The Tetrahedron of the Sun points backward

The Tetrahedron of the Earth points forward

Men/male: The Tetrahedron of the Sun points forward.

The Tetrahedron of the Earth points backward

General explanation of the first 6 breaths

During the **first in-breath** you should at the same time:

Heart: Feel love filling your heart

Mudra: turn the palms of the hands upwards, allowing the thumb and first finger to touch. The other fingers should not touch anything

Mind: Experience the Tetrahedron of the Sun (the upper). It starts about a "hand's width" above your head – the peak pointing backward on women and forward on men. Visualise the Tetrahedron of the Sun filling with white light. Feel how it is being filled with this energy. The base of the Tetrahedron is as wide as you are when you hold your arms out-stretched from the body plus an additional couple of centimetres on each side (we are our own measure stocks).

During the <u>first out-breath</u> you should at the same time:

Heart: Feel love

Mudra: the same as when breathing in

Mind: Experience the Tetrahedron of the Earth

(the lower) It starts about a "hand's width" underneath your feet if you are standing – the peak pointing forward on women and backward on men. Visualise the Tetrahedron of the Earth filling with white light. Feel how it is being filled with this energy.

Breathing: Whilst exhaling, simultaneously as you are performing the eye movements mentioned below, become conscious of a triangular form which exists inside the Tetrahedron of the Earth being sent downward, cleansing your inner being as it does so. Visualise all your blockages flowing out through the peak down to the Mother Earth. It

57

happens very quickly, often in the form of a lightening flash. Know that Mother Earth can easily cleanse this for you.

Body: Close your eyes or keep them open – you choose but the following exercise should be performed simultaneously as the triangular form is cleansing your body: cross your eyes slowly, look up (not strained), look down as quickly as you can.

Breaths 2-6

You perform all parts as in the first in-breath except one. The only part that differs is your Mudra.

In-breath 2 and out-breath: Mudra: turn the palms of the hands upwards, allowing the thumb and middle finger to touch. The other fingers should not touch anything.

In-breath 3 and out-breath: Mudra: turn the palms of the hands upwards, allowing the thumb and the third finger to touch. The other finger should not touch anything.

In-breath 4 and out-breath: Mudra: turn the palms of the hands upwards, allowing the thumb and little finger to touch. The other fingers should not touch anything.

In-breath 5 and out-breath: Mudra: turn the palms of the hands upwards, allowing the thumb and first finger to touch. The other fingers should not touch anything.

In-breath 6 and out-breath: Mudra: turn the palms of the hands upwards, allowing the thumb and the middle finger to touch. The other fingers should not touch anything.

I suggest you practise each individual part before you attempt to do them all at once. Start with the eye movements. They are meant to awaken your cell memories because you already have this knowledge lodged in your cells. The eye movements are designed to activate the correct memories.

When you feel comfortable with the eye movements I suggest you continue with the Mudra. You will soon discover that they are fairly self-evident.

Now comes the time to understand and feel the Tetrahedron of the Sun and thereafter the Tetrahedron of the Earth. Be particularly careful to turn them in the correct direction depending on whether you are a woman or a man.

Then try to do it all at once. It is perfectly alright to have a piece of paper in front of you from which you can read the instructions. Initially I did this myself for as long as it was necessary.

Last in the book is an appendix that compiles Markaba activation,
please use it when training

Exercises for chapter 3

Continue to anchor your Heart into the Earth and the Sun. It is good to start each day with this meditation.

Do the meditation to find The Sacred Space of the Heart at least once a week, about 15-20 minutes each time.

Practice the first 6 breathing practices until you really know them.

Chapter 4 – The Sphere

By now I hope you are beginning to understand how the first 6 breaths within your Merkaba work. When you have practised enough times your body will help you remember the different parts you perform during each breath. Do your exercises with joy. This is one of the most important light bodies we need as human beings. Furthermore, your Merkaba will be the one to best assist you during the forthcoming Shift which many of us believe will happen.

During chapter 4 you will learn the breaths 7 – 13. This time there are new parts of your Merkaba for you to understand. I will start with a general explanation of the different parts.

Enjoy!
// Susanne

During this part of the Merkaba activation you will no longer need to visualise the Tetrahedron star. Instead you will now work with your Prana tube and create your own sphere.

The Sphere

Leonardo Da Vinci has created a so called "norm", i.e. a drawing showing the proportions of a human being. If you have some knowledge of Sacred Geometry and the Merkaba, you will soon realize that this was also the knowledge of Leonardo Da Vinci. In this drawing he shows essential parts of the Sacred Geometry, the Golden Mean, Fibonacci and the Merkaba field. If you want to study this further, I would recommend you use the Internet.

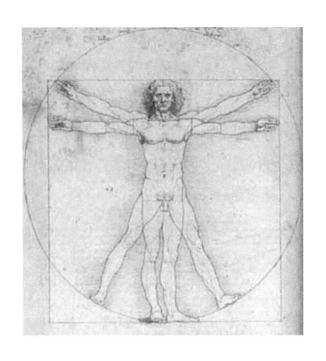

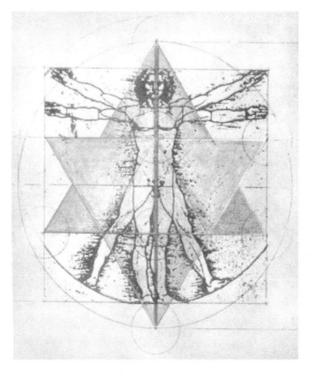

In this picture it is easier to see the various parts but
what is most important right now is the Prana tube

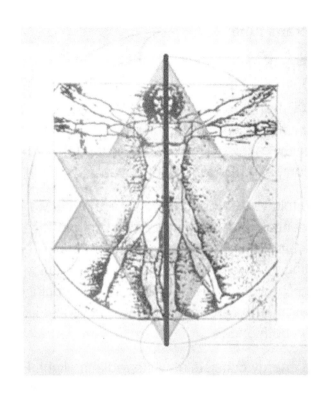

The Prana tube

Your Prana tube starts in the upper part of the Tetrahedron of the Sun and ends in the lower part of the Tetrahedron of the Earth. Prana is flowing through the tube from the fourth dimension above and below to meet in your body. Where this energy flow comes from we will soon reveal.

I have told you before and do so again that we have all essential measurements within our bodies. Your Prana tube is as wide as the ring formed between your fingers when your thumb meets your middle finger. The tube starts and finishes in the point of the Tetrahedron star and ends with a crystal-like point in both ends.

Prana energy consists of white radiating light. Prana is life energy, the energy which exists in all things.

Start practising when you have read the full instruction and feel that you are beginning to understand it.

Part 2 of the Merkaba activation

The 7th breath – in-breath:

Heart: Feel love

Mind: Visualise your Prana tube, see how a white light is flowing from both ends and meet in the tube at the level of the navel. During the in-breath you observe how the point where the flow of energy meets expands and starts to create a small Prana sphere (ball) of blue frequency/energy.

Mudra: The palms of the hands point upwards, the thumb and first and middle finger meet.

Breathing: Yogi breath 7 seconds slow in-breath through the nose.

The 7th breath – out-breath:

Heart: Feel love

Mind: See how the Prana sphere expands slowly. At full exhalation it is about 20 cm in size.

Mudra: Same as before

Breathing: Yogi breath 7 seconds slow out-breath through the nose

The 8th breath – in-breath:

Heart: Truth

Mind: See how the Prana sphere continues to grow

Mudra: Same as before

Breathing: Yogi breath 7 seconds slow in-breath through the nose

The 8th breath – out-breath:

Heart: Truth

Mind: See how the Prana sphere expands and expands. At full exhalation it will reach maximum size and is then about 40 cm large.

Mudra: Same as before

Breathing: Yogi breath 7 seconds slow out-breath through the nose

The 9th breath – in-breath:

Heart: Beauty

Mind: See how the Prana sphere increases in energy and strength

Mudra: Same as before

Breathing: Yogi breath 7 seconds slow in-breath through the nose

The 9th breath – out-breath:

Heart: Beauty

Mind: See how the Prana sphere increases to full energy and strength

Mudra: Same as before

Breathing: Yogi breath 7 seconds slow out-breath through the nose

Now we are at the next step of the light body. The time has come to form the Golden Sphere.

The Sphere

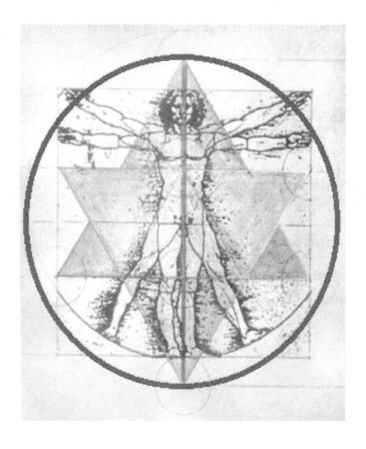

During the 10th breath the Sphere will be created. This will take place during the out-breath and this out-breath will be different.

Breathe slowly as before for 7 seconds (while following the instructions).

Out-breath: This is called **Powerful out-breath**: Exhale the air through a narrow gap between your lips. Do it very quickly and powerfully. Feel how the stomach muscles and rib cage are activated during the out-breath.

At the same time as you are exhaling a Golden Sphere is created from your Prana sphere. This new Golden Sphere is growing quickly in strength until it surrounds you completely – see the size in the picture above.

The 10th breath – in-breath:

Heart: Trust

Mind: The Prana sphere is now reaching its full capacity and strength while changing its frequency/colour from blue to golden. The sphere becomes a Golden Sphere by the energy of the Sun

Mudra: Same as before

Breathing: Yogi breath 7 seconds slow in-breath through the nose

The 10th breath – out-breath:

Heart: Trust

Mind: See how the Prana sphere now quickly expands at the same pace as the out-breath and how quickly it grows to become a Golden Sphere surrounding you completely.

Mudra: Same as before

Breathing: Powerful out-breath

The following breathing helps to stabilise the Prana tube and sphere.

Breath 11, 12 and 13

You can now relax and detach from the visualisation

Continue to breathe in and out slowly – 7 seconds – through the nose (Yogi breathing)

Keep the same Mudra

The only difference between these breaths is the feeling in your Heart.

Breath 11, both in and out

Heart: Harmony

Breath 12, both in and out

Heart: Peace

Breath 13, both in and out

Heart: Reverence for God

After the 13th breath the Golden Sphere is now stabilised and you now have two clear spheres, the inner and the outer.

I enclose a summary of breaths 7 – 13 in the end of this book to make it easier for you to follow it when you are practising. There is no problem with you reading while you are doing the exercise. Your body will soon be assisting you to remember all parts of the activation.

Exercises for chapter 4

Continue to anchor your Heart into the Earth and the Sun. It is good to start each day with this meditation.

Do the meditation to find The Sacred Space of the Heart at least once a week, about 15-20 minutes each time.

Practice the first 6 breathing practices in your Merkaba

Practice the following 7-13 breaths in your Merkaba until you understand them.

Chapter 5

Now comes the time for activating the whole of the Merkaba meditation. You will learn how to link together the Crown, the Sacred Space of the Heart and your Merkaba.

You will also learn how to programme your Merkaba.

When you have learnt all parts of these meditations it will not take more than 20 minutes per day or 5 minutes if you are in a hurry, to maintain your Merkaba. I believe that you have time for this and also you want to do it.

Enjoy!

Part 3 of the Merkaba activation

The 14th breath

This is one of the most important breaths. You are now going to anchor your Prana sphere into your Heart.

The 14th breath – in-breath:

Heart: Love

Mind: Move the Prana meeting point and your inner Prana Sphere from the Navel chakra up to the Heart chakra

Mudra and body: This applies to the rest of the Merkaba meditation

Women: Palms of the hands facing upwards. Right hand is placed over the left hand, the thumbs touch each other slightly

Men: Palms of the hands facing upwards. Left hand is placed over the right hand, the thumbs touch each other slightly

Breathing: Yogi breath 7 seconds slow in-breath through the nose

The 14th breath – out-breath:

Heart: Love

Mind: During the out-breath you will anchor your Prana Sphere and meeting point in your Heart chakra

Mudra: Same as before

Breathing: Yogi breath 7 seconds slow out-breath through your nose

The 14th breath changes your whole energy field. You will find it easier to reach your Heart and live with love in a balanced way.

When you have anchored your Prana flow in your Heart chakra you will also find it easier to reach the Fourth Dimension.

Part 4 of the Merkaba activation

The last three breaths will activate your Merkaba. I will first of all describe the process in words and then with clear instructions.

Please note – It is the same Mudra as in breath 14. Therefore I will not repeat it in the following exercises.

The 15th breath will start rotating your Merkaba in the correct way. You will soon understand that there are three Tetrahedron stars surrounding you. They are exactly the same size but have different energies.

The first Tetrahedron star which is closest to your body is connected to your physical body. This star will remain stationary the whole time.

The middle Tetrahedron star is masculine and shall be rotated to the left.

The outer Tetrahedron star is feminine and shall be rotated to the right.

The 16th Breath

When all the stars are rotating in the correct way we will make them rotate according to the Fibonacci numbers. It will happen when we call out the correct number. When the stars are rotating according to this sequence (34/21), a disc will be created starting from your root chakra and expanding outwards – about 17 meters (55 ft).

The 17th Breath

Here we aim to find the correct total speed of the whole of your Merkaba (9/10 part of the speed of light).

Now you have an overview of the last breaths. You will find the correct instruction on the next page.

As previously, I am attaching a summary instruction, this time with all the 17 breaths of the Merkaba.

The 15ᵗʰ Breath – In-breath:

Heart: Pure Love

Mind: Become conscious of the fact that the **first Tetrahedron star** which is closest to your body is connected to your physical body. It will remain **completely stationary** the whole time. The **middle Tetrahedron star** is masculine and it shall **be rotated to the left**. The **outer Tetrahedron star** is feminine and shall be **rotated to the right**.

Breathing: Yogi breath 7 seconds slow in-breath through the nose

The 15ᵗʰ Breath – Out-breath:

Heart: Pure Love

Mind: Think: same speed! The two outer stars will start to rotate, each one in its own way while the inner star remains stationary.

Breathing: Powerful out-breath: Exhale the air through a narrow gap between your lips. Do it very quickly and powerfully. Feel how the stomach muscles and rib cage are activated during the out-breath.

The 16ᵗʰ Breath – In-breath:

Heart: Pure Love

Mind: Tell yourself in a determined way: 34/21 (think 34 to 21)

Breathing: Yogi breath 7 seconds slow in-breath through the nose

The 16ᵗʰ Breath – Out-breath:

Heart: Pure Love

Mind: When the Tetrahedron stars rotate at exactly the same speed a disc is formed from the base of the spine. The disc is ejected outwards to about 17 meters (55 ft) surrounding you.

Breathing: Powerful out-breath: Exhale the air through a narrow gap between your lips. Do it very quickly and powerfully. Feel how the stomach muscles and rib cage are activated during the out-breath.

The 17th Breath – In-breath:

Heart: Pure Love

Mind: Tell yourself : Nine tenths of the speed of light

Breathing: Yogi breath 7 seconds slow in-breath through the nose

The 17th Breath – Out-breath:

Heart: Pure Love

Mind: The Merkaba is stabilised at 9/10 the speed of light

Breathing: Powerful out-breath: Exhale the air through a narrow gap between your lips. Do it very quickly and powerfully. Feel how the stomach muscles and rib cage are activated during the out-breath.

You may stay in this meditation as long as you wish – enjoy!

End the Merkaba meditation in a way comfortable to you. One way is to bring your hands together and place them on your heart. You may also express heartfelt gratitude or "Namaste" in Sanskrit which means gratitude from the depth of my heart or more correctly:

"I greet and honour the Divine within you which is the Divine within me"

 **Congratulations!** Now you have the complete knowledge of the 17 breaths in the activation of the Merkaba. It is now up to you to practise, first the last 14-17 breaths and then perform the whole meditation in one go.

When you can perform all 17 breaths in sequence, then your Merkaba is activated. To keep your Merkaba activated you must, under a long period, perform the Merkaba meditation daily but when you know the meditation it will not take more than 5 minutes to complete it. Use this time sequence each day – you are worth it!

In order to anchor the Merkaba permanently you need to perform the meditation during a long period, maybe up to two years. The most common obstacle that many people find is to listen to the ego which tells you that "your Merkaba is anchored now". This may occur after just a couple of months. Continue the meditation until you are absolutely sure. The Merkaba will stop rotating after about 48 hours unless it is anchored so you can miss a day but do not do it too often.

The most common misunderstandings

To believe that the Tetrahedron star splits so that the Tetrahedron of the Sun and the Tetrahedron of the Earth should rotate in different directions. The truth it that there are three different Tetrahedron stars and they shall rotate each in its own direction: the inner, the Tetrahedron of the Body, remains stationary, next is the masculine Tetrahedron star which rotates to the left and the outer is the feminine Tetrahedron star which rotates to the right.

To stop doing your Merkaba activation too early as your ego has made you believe you are complete.

To be careless with the details – all parts are equally important.

If it´s difficult to visualise the correct size of the Tetrahedron star – too big or too small. If you have this problem, stand in your place of meditation, stretch your arms out as far away from the body as possible – rotate round once – this is how big (wide) your Tetrahedron star is. You can mark the size of the ring on the floor or place a piece of string or similar around to make it easier for you to find your size.

That the disc expanding outwards during the 16th breath ends up in the wrong place. It shall start at the lower part of your spine. If you sit on the floor the disc will start at the level of the floor.

To view yourself being inside the Merkaba but you are looking at the picture from outside. You must be inside your Merkaba when you view yourself being there.

Your Merkaba from a distance

Your Merkaba close up

Use your Merkaba

When you have learnt the Merkaba meditation and you find it quick and safe to use, you can then use your Merkaba in various ways.

To meet your Higher Self:
One of the advantages of the Merkaba is to gain a clear and real contact with your Higher Self.

Your Higher Self is the aspect of you which has full knowledge of all parts of you and remembers everything you have experienced. You can ask any questions you want to your Higher Self and always receive answers – maybe not always what you expect but in one way or another you will receive an answer. Sometimes the answer will come immediately as you ask the question or you may receive the answer through a newspaper article or from someone who just wants to share something with you. In one way or another you will receive an answer.

When you are in your Merkaba and have done the whole meditation, you simply ask your Higher Self to enter – and your Higher Self is there instantaneously. To be sure, you should ask the question: "Are you my Higher Self?" It may appear unnecessary but it could happen that your lower self enters in instead – your lower self is more attached to your body - the earthly part of you which has desires and knowledge of the body. It is not unusual that the lower self wants sweets or deeds purely for self-satisfaction. It may not be wrong but it is not necessarily what is best for you. If you want answers to your questions they must come from the knowledge of your Higher Self.

To programme the Merkaba

You can create an outer Merkaba and place it over a well, for example, to keep the water clean. Or surround your home with the Merkaba to cleanse the energies. You will decide where to place the Prana tube – the outer limits of the disc must not exceed the limits of your property or your apartment (you must not extend your Merkaba to someone else's property).

You create this outer Merkaba at the same time as you create your own personal Merkaba. See how the various parts are lodged in the correct place as you are completing your own Merkaba. You need to maintain this Merkaba from time to time to ensure it rotates correctly but the water in the well or the energy in your home will forever remain clean.

You programme the Merkaba by expressing your intention for its use. Do not worry about details but just determine that this Merkaba will have this function – and it will work.

Self-teaching Merkaba

When you get to know your Merkaba you will also learn more. The Merkaba itself will teach you. Your knowledge will increase in step with the anchoring of your Merkaba.

Unity-Breath

There is a breathing exercise called Unity-Breath. This breathing technique gives you a conscious experience of being in contact with All-That-Is.

Sit comfortably with the feet on the floor if you can, turn the palms of the hands down

Anchor your Heart in the Earth and the Sun

Activate your Merkaba

Breathe deeply a couple of times

Keep your focus on your Prana tube and be conscious of both ends of the tube

See how the Prana flow increases and fills the whole of your body. Feel how the Prana energy fills your body with a conscious contact with the Divine energy

Towards a Higher Consciousness

Now you have all the tools necessary to reach a Higher Consciousness.

You start by anchoring your Heart into the Earth and the Sun

Do your Merkaba meditation

Go to the Sacred Space of your Heart

Push the tongue up against the roof of the mouth and create contact with the Crown and Third Eye

When you have performed this meditation enough times you will experience how an energy, often a shade of green in colour, descends down through your Crown chakra to the Pineal gland and activates this gland to an entirely new level.

What you have to do now is to direct/turn this activation/energy forward – through your Third Eye and out – to meet the furthermost point of your Crown. The whole Crown will then be lit up and from this moment on your Third Eye is open and you are anchored in a higher state of consciousness.

In this way you will use your Higher Consciousness through your Heart. You will then develop yourself in a loving way, without ego. This is the best way for all people and the Earth herself.

To start the day by anchoring your Heart in the Earth and in the Sun, activate your Merkaba through the 17 breaths and then find your Heart place to meditate - this is the best way to reach your Higher Consciousness and connect with your inner knowledge. You will find a peace in everyday life and in the life that you might not have been able to experience before.

When you have finished meditating, stay with your consciousness in your most holy place in your heart - complete the meditation - open your eyes. In this way, you learn to live from your heart every day.

With love and light // Susanne Jönsson

The author Susanne Jönsson answer questions about the book as time permits, contact her by email at

support@soulheartjourney.com

The meditation to the Heart is available in videos and mp3 files for download if you think that will help, it will guide you first how to anchor your heart in the Sun and in the Earth and then how you find your sacred space in your heart.

You'll find them on: www. soulheartjourney.com

Do you prefer to do these exercises guided on videos or Mp3 files? You'll find most of them on:
www.soulheartjourney.com

Soul&Heart
Journey School

Part 1 of the Merkaba activation

Breath 1 - 6

Breath 1 in:
Heart: Feel love

Mudra: turn the palms of the hands upwards, allowing the thumb and first finger to touch. The other fingers should not touch anything

Mind: Experience the Tetrahedron of the Sun (the upper).

Breath 1 out:
Heart: Feel love

Mudra: the same as when breathing in

Mind: Experience the Tetrahedron of the Earth

Breathing: Whilst exhaling, simultaneously as you are performing the eye movements mentioned below, become conscious of a triangular form which exists inside the Tetrahedron of the Earth being sent downward, cleansing your inner being as it does so.

Visualise all your blockages flowing out through the peak down to the Mother Earth.

Body: Cross your eyes slowly, look up (not strained), look down as quickly as you can.

Breaths 2-6

You perform all parts as in the first in-breath except one. The only part that differs is your Mudra.

In-breath 2 and out-breath: Mudra: turn the palms of the hands upwards, allowing the thumb and middle finger to touch. The other fingers should not touch anything.

In-breath 3 and out-breath: Mudra: turn the palms of the hands upwards, allowing the thumb and the third finger to touch. The other finger should not touch anything.

In-breath 4 and out-breath: Mudra: turn the palms of the hands upwards, allowing the thumb and little finger to touch. The other fingers should not touch anything.

In-breath 5 and out-breath: Mudra: turn the palms of the hands upwards, allowing the thumb and first finger to touch. The other fingers should not touch anything.

In-breath 6 and out-breath: Mudra: turn the palms of the hands upwards, allowing the thumb and the middle finger to touch. The other fingers should not touch anything.

Part 2 of the Merkaba activation

Breath 7 - 3

The 7th breath – in-breath:

Heart: Feel love

Mind: Visualise your Prana tube, see a small Prana sphere is growing, just behind your navel.

Mudra: The palms of the hands point upwards, the thumb and first and middle finger meet.

Breathing: Yogi breath 7 seconds slow in-breath through the nose.

The 7th breath – out-breath:

Heart: Feel love

Mind: See how the Prana sphere expands slowly. At full exhalation it is about 20 cm in size.

Mudra: Same as before

Breathing: Yogi breath 7 seconds slow out-breath through the nose

The 8th breath – in-breath:

Heart: Truth

Mind: See how the Prana sphere continues to grow

Mudra: Same as before

Breathing: Yogi breath 7 seconds slow in-breath through the nose

The 8th breath – out-breath:

Heart: Truth

Mind: See how the Prana sphere expands and expands. At full exhalation it will reach maximum size and is then about 40 cm large.

Mudra: Same as before

Breathing: Yogi breath 7 seconds slow out-breath through the nose

The 9ᵗʰ breath – in-breath:

Heart: Beauty

Mind: See how the Prana sphere increases in energy and strength

Mudra: Same as before

Breathing: Yogi breath 7 seconds slow in-breath through the nose

The 9ᵗʰ breath – out-breath:

Heart: Beauty

Mind: See how the Prana sphere increases to full energy and strength

Mudra: Same as before

Breathing: Yogi breath 7 seconds slow out-breath through the nose.

The 10th breath – in-breath:

Heart: Trust

Mind: The Prana sphere is now reaching its full capacity and strength while changing its frequency/colour from blue to golden. The sphere becomes a Golden Sphere by the energy of the Sun

Mudra: Same as before

Breathing: Yogi breath 7 seconds slow in-breath through the nose

The 10th breath – out-breath:

Heart: Trust

Mind: See how the Prana sphere now quickly expands at the same pace as the out-breath and how quickly it grows to become a Golden Sphere surrounding you completely.

Mudra: Same as before

Breathing: Powerful out-breath

The following breathing helps to stabilise the Prana tube and sphere.

Breath 11, 12 and 13

You can now relax and detach from the visualisation

Continue to breathe in and out slowly – 7 seconds – through the nose (Yogi breathing)

Keep the same Mudra

The only difference between these breaths is the feeling in your Heart.

Breath 11, both in and out
Heart: Harmony

Breath 12, both in and out
Heart: Peace

Breath 13, both in and out
Heart: Reverence for God

After the 13th breath the Golden Sphere is now stabilised and you now have two clear spheres, the inner and the outer.

Part 3 of the Merkaba activation

The 14th breath

This is one of the most important breaths. You are now going to anchor your Prana sphere into your Heart.

The 14th breath – in-breath:

Heart: Love

Mind: Move the Prana meeting point and your inner Prana Sphere from the Navel chakra up to the Heart chakra

Mudra and body: This applies to the rest of the Merkaba meditation

Women: Palms of the hands facing upwards. Right hand is placed over the left hand, the thumbs touch each other slightly

Men: Palms of the hands facing upwards. Left hand is placed over the right hand, the thumbs touch each other slightly

Breathing: Yogi breath 7 seconds slow in-breath through the nose

The 14th breath – out-breath:

Heart: Love

Mind: During the out-breath you will anchor your Prana Sphere and meeting point in your Heart chakra

Mudra: Same as before

Breathing: Yogi breath 7 seconds slow out-breath through your nose

Part 4 of the Merkaba activation

The 15th Breath – In-breath:

Heart: Pure Love

Mind: Become conscious of the fact that the **first Tetrahedron star** which is closest to your body is connected to <u>your physical body</u>. It will remain **completely stationary** the whole time. The **middle Tetrahedron star** is <u>masculine</u> and it shall **be rotated to the left**. The **outer Tetrahedron star** is <u>feminine</u> and shall be **rotated to the right**.

Breathing: Yogi breath 7 seconds slow in-breath through the nose

The 15th Breath – Out-breath:

Heart: Pure Love

Mind: Think: same speed! The two outer stars will start to rotate, each one in its own way while the inner star remains stationary.

Breathing: Powerful out-breath: Exhale the air through a narrow gap between your lips. Do it very quickly and powerfully. Feel how the stomach muscles and rib cage are activated during the out-breath.

The 16ᵗʰ Breath – In-breath:

Heart: Pure Love

Mind: Tell yourself in a determined way: 34/21 (think 34 to 21)

Breathing: Yogi breath 7 seconds slow in-breath through the nose

The 16ᵗʰ Breath – Out-breath:

Heart: Pure Love

Mind: When the Tetrahedron stars rotate at exactly the same speed a disc is formed from the base of the spine. The disc is ejected outwards to about 17 meters (55 ft) surrounding you.

Breathing: Powerful out-breath: Exhale the air through a narrow gap between your lips. Do it very quickly and powerfully. Feel how the stomach muscles and rib cage are activated during the out-breath.

The 17th Breath – In-breath:

Heart: Pure Love

Mind: Tell yourself : Nine tenths of the speed of light

Breathing: Yogi breath 7 seconds slow in-breath through the nose

The 17th Breath – Out-breath:

Heart: Pure Love

Mind: The Merkaba is stabilised at 9/10 the speed of light

Breathing: Powerful out-breath: Exhale the air through a narrow gap between your lips. Do it very quickly and powerfully. Feel how the stomach muscles and rib cage are activated during the out-breath.

Made in the USA
Monee, IL
16 May 2023

33843572R20066